For the woman who has ever felt like she is too much
and yet, never enough.
For the one who was told to be small, to be quiet,
to be anything other than wild, radiant, untamed, and fully herself.
For the one who has forgotten her power,
her magic, her divine inheritance.
You were never meant to shrink.
You were always meant to shine.
This book is your reminder,
your permission slip,
your rebirth.
May you rise, may you reclaim, may you remember.
With love, fire, and unwavering belief in you
X Cailin

# Disclaimer

This book is intended for informational and inspirational purposes only. The author is not a medical, legal, or financial professional, and the content within should not be taken as professional advice. If you require guidance in these areas, please consult the appropriate expert. The words in this book are not spells, not prophecies, not rules—they are invitations. Each ritual, story, and practice is designed to guide you back to yourself. You do not need to follow them all. You do not need to believe in them all. You only need to trust what feels right to you. You are your own greatest teacher. The goddesses are simply here to remind you.

Copyright © April 2025 by Cailin Cooper
All rights reserved.

No part of this book may be reproduced, distributed, or transmitted in any form or by any means, including photocopying, recording, or other electronic or mechanical methods, without the prior written permission of the author, except in the case of brief quotations embodied in critical reviews and certain other noncommercial uses permitted by copyright law. For permission requests, write to the publisher, addressed "Attention: Permissions Coordinator," at the address below.
Cooper Delivered
info@cooperdelivered.com.au

*Awakening the Goddess Within A Journey of Power, Beauty & Transformation*

## THE INVITATION TO AWAKEN

Dear reader,

Have you ever felt like there was something more? Something unspoken, unseen power humming beneath your skin, waiting for the moment to rise? This book is not just a guide. It is a mirror, a portal, an awakening. Inside these pages, you will meet thirteen goddesses, each with her own myth, her own struggles, her own transformation. These are not just stories from ancient times; these are the echoes of who you have been, who you are, and who you are becoming. Some days, you will feel like Aphrodite bold, magnetic, irresistible. Other days, you will be Skadi cold, untouchable, fierce in your solitude. You may be Yhi, stepping into your first breath of awakening, or Hecate, standing at the crossroads of fate. But remember this: You are not just one goddess—you are all of them. Let this book be your companion, your whisper of wisdom in the dark, your reminder that you are never alone.

Turn the page, my love. It is time.

# The Awakening

There has always been a whisper in the back of your mind. A pulse beneath your skin. A feeling you cannot name—but have never been able to shake.

It was there when you stood in front of the mirror, searching for the spark in your reflection. It was there when the world told you to be smaller, quieter, easier to hold. It was there in the quiet hours, between waking and dreaming, when your soul still remembered what your mind had tried to forget.

You were never meant to be small.

You were never meant to be silent.

You were never meant to forget.

Something inside you has been waiting.

And that is why you are here.

They will tell you that goddesses are myths. That they belong to another time, another world. That they were carved into stone, painted onto temple walls, their names spoken in prayers that have long since faded into silence.

But that is a lie.

Goddesses were never just myths.

They were women who refused to be erased. They were forces that could not be ignored. They were beings that lived so fiercely, so unapologetically, that the world could only explain their power by calling them divine.

And here is the secret: they are still here.

They exist in every woman who has ever claimed her voice back.

In every woman who has ever chosen herself over what was expected.

In every woman who has burned down the cage she was put in and built something greater from the ashes.

They are in you.

They have always been in you.

This book is not about learning them.

It is about remembering them.

Because a goddess is not born from soft hands and safe places.

The world does not simply create goddesses.

They are born in the breaking.

In the moments where everything you thought you were falls away—until only power remains.

Aphrodite was not born in the gentle tide—she rose from the violent sea, from destruction and loss, a creation of the broken and the forgotten.

Hecate does not wait at the crossroads because it is safe—she waits because it is where the lost go to be found.

Pele does not just dance in the fire—she becomes it, consuming everything that cannot withstand her heat.

You do not awaken your inner goddess when life is soft and kind.

You awaken her when the world tries to silence you, and you rise anyway.

But what if everything we've been told about power, about goddesses, about fate is only part of the truth?

Because we have been taught that goddesses are different from us.

That they were divine, untouchable, something beyond our reach.

But what if they weren't?

What if they were just women?

Women who were too powerful to be forgotten.

Women who defied the rules of their time and were given crowns instead of cages.

Women who could not be erased—so they were made into something larger than life.

What if goddesses were never divine at all?

What if power was never given—but simply taken by those who refused to live without it?

Because across every land, every people, every civilisation, there has always been a goddess.

They burned her temples, erased her name from history, rewrote her stories to make her softer, smaller, easier to control.

But she survived.

She always survives.

- In Japan, Amaterasu is the sun itself, the light that brings life to the world. In Egypt, Isis is the great mother, the healer, the queen of magic.
- In Greece, Persephone walks between death and life, showing us how to survive the dark.
- Among the Norse, Freyja is both lover and warrior, proving that we do not have to choose between beauty and strength.
- In Indigenous Australia, Yhi awakens the world, bringing warmth and breath to everything that lives. The divine feminine has always existed.

Still, she survived.

Still, we survived.

And now, we rise. You were never just a woman. You were never just a name, a body, a whisper in the dark. You were always meant to be more. You were always meant to rise.

And now, it is time.

There is no single way to move through these pages. This is not a book to be read once and set aside.

It is a guide, a ritual, a conversation between you and the goddesses who have walked before you. Some parts will call to you immediately turn to them. Some pages will hold lessons you are not yet ready for return to them when the time is right.

This book is not about consuming knowledge. It is about remembering something you have always known. Inside, you will find:

- Myths reimagined stories of goddesses who shaped the world and refused to be forgotten.
- The Mystery of Who They Are Today a glimpse into what these goddesses would become if they lived in our world.
- Power Practices & Rituals ways to embody their energy in your daily life.
- Reflections & Journaling Prompts spaces for you to explore how their power lives in you.

You do not need to start at the beginning. You do not need to follow a path that is not yours. If you are at a crossroads, turn to Hecate. If your fire has been dimmed, Pele will reignite it. If you are seeking love, Aphrodite will remind you to start with yourself.

Read slowly.
Breathe deeply.

And when you are ready step into the first light.


Turn the page.

# BEFORE THE DAWN, THERE WAS ONLY DARKNESS

Before the first river carved the land, before the trees swayed in the wind, before the dawn kissed the horizon.
There was only darkness.
And then, there was me.
I am the first light, the warmth that touches your skin after the longest night. I am the breath that fills your lungs as you wake, the first step on a new path, the spark that ignites everything.
I am awakening, becoming, transformation.
I am the promise that you were always meant to shine.

# I AM TOLD MY STORY GOES...

In Australian Aboriginal mythology, I am Yhi, the Goddess of Creation, Light, and Growth. I belong to the land, to the sky, to the breath of the earth itself. They say I slept in the darkness for eternity, until one day, I heard a call a whisper, a longing, a desire for life.
So I opened my eyes.
And with that single act, the world began.
My light touched the void, and the shadows fled before me. I walked the land, and wherever my feet touched, flowers bloomed, rivers swelled, creatures stirred in the earth. I gave life to all things. I was the first sunrise, the first spark of warmth, the first fire in the soul of every living being. But I was not simply a gentle light.
My heat brought change.
My presence demanded transformation.
The creatures I created had to wake, had to move, had to grow. Some feared what my light revealed. Some longed to stay in the comfort of the shadows. But I do not wait for permission to rise.
I burn away hesitation.
I shatter the illusion of smallness.
I call all things into their fullest form. And when my work was done, I rose into the sky, becoming the sun itself, watching over the world, reminding you
You were not made for darkness.
You were made to wake up.
To rise. To stretch. To step into something greater than you ever imagined.
You have been asleep for too long, my love. The waiting is over.
It is time to become.

# THE MYSTERY OF YHI – WHO IS SHE TODAY?

I walk this earth today, unseen but ever present.
I rise with the sun.
I awaken the weary.
I lift those who have been told to stay small. I do not wait to be invited in.
I have always belonged.
I do not ask for permission to shine.
I have always been light.
I do not shrink for the comfort of others—I was born to take up space.
Today, I guide with breath.
With movement.
With light.
You will find me where the earth meets the sky, where bare feet press into warm soil, where voices carry on the wind, where the breath of the land itself moves through us.
A quiet room bathed in golden light. The scent of eucalyptus and warm earth. The hum of a world that remembers. She stands before you, tall, unshaken, steady as the rising sun. Her skin carries the warmth of generations, Her voice carries the wisdom of those who came before.
Close your eyes, she says, her voice smooth as sunlight filtering through leaves. Breathe in. The air fills your lungs, expanding your chest, waking something deep inside you.
Now exhale. Let go of the weight, the hesitation, the fear.
You do. And now, open your eyes.
You blink. The world is brighter. The edges are sharper.
The colours richer.
The sounds more alive than before.
She smiles.
You are ready.
You are Yhi.
You have always belonged to the light.
And now, it is time to rise.

# YHI'S RITUALS: AWAKENING, GROWTH & THE FIRST STEP FORWARD

To walk with Yhi is to step into your light to shake off the sleep of doubt and hesitation, and embrace the fire of your own becoming.

## RITUAL 1: THE FIRST LIGHT MEDITATION (For New Beginnings & Clarity)

Symbolism: The rising sun represents the moment of awakening, the choice to begin again.

**What You Need:**
A quiet space facing the sunrise
A deep breath, taken with full presence
A single affirmation spoken aloud

**How to Use:**
Stand in the light of the rising sun, feeling its warmth against your skin.
Take one deep breath, imagining yourself filling with energy, clarity, and purpose.
Whisper: "I awaken. I rise. I am ready."
Feel the shift inside you the knowledge that from this moment on, everything changes.

## RITUAL 2: THE BUSH MEDICINE AWAKENING BALM (For Vitality & Radiance)

Inspired by ancient Aboriginal botanical healing, this ritual restores the body and awakens the senses.

**Ingredients:**
1 tsp lemon myrtle powder (clarity, focus, awakening of the senses)
½ tsp wattleseed powder (nourishment, connection to the land, gentle exfoliation)
1 tbsp macadamia oil (softens, restores, and protects the skin)
A few drops of eucalyptus oil (clears the mind, brings deep breath and focus)

**How to Use:**
Mix ingredients into a smooth paste.
Apply gently to your face, feeling the warmth of the land beneath your skin, the energy stirring in your blood.
Close your eyes and inhale deeply—smell the lemon myrtle, the wattle, the crisp touch of eucalyptus. Let it clear your mind.
Whisper: "I awaken to my own strength. I rise like the first light. I am alive, I am here, I am ready."
Rinse with cool water, standing in the sunlight, feeling the shift within you.

## WHAT MESSAGE DOES YHI WHISPER TO YOU?

Breathe, my love.
Feel the air filling your lungs, the warmth of the sun on your skin.
You are not meant to live half-asleep, moving through your days without truly seeing, truly feeling. You are not meant to fade into the background of your own life
You were born to rise.
To open your eyes and see the world for what it is a place waiting for you to step into your power.
To step into the light.
I have given life to the land, to the creatures, to the very breath of the wind.
And now, I give that power to you.
So, my love, what will you do with it?
You are no longer waiting.
You are no longer lost.
You are no longer asleep.

She places a warm hand over your heart, her voice no longer a whisper but a declaration.

You are awake
And now, my love, you begin.

*I shine with divine radiance, my light is powerful, and I illuminate the world.*

Amaterasu

The Goddess of the Sun

# BEFORE THE DAWN, THERE WAS SHADOW

You are not here to be unseen.
You are not here to be small.
You are the sunrise.
I am light, the golden warmth that spills across the land, the brilliance that floods the sky, the sun that returns unwavering, unbroken after every long night.
When the world is dim, when you forget who you are, when the shadows whisper that it is safer to disappear, I remind you.
You were never meant to stay hidden.

# I AM TOLD MY STORY GOES...

In Japanese mythology, I am Amaterasu-ōmikami (天照大神)—the Shinto Sun Goddess, the most revered deity in Japan's ancient belief system. I rule Takamagahara, the High Celestial Plain, where spirits and gods reside.
I am the divine ancestor of the Japanese Imperial family, honored as the goddess of light, warmth, and prosperity. My name means "Great Divinity Who Illuminates the Heavens", for it is I who bring the day, I who ensure the balance of life. They worship me at Ise Grand Shrine (Ise Jingū), where the Sacred Mirror of Amaterasu—one of Japan's three imperial regalia—is said to reside. A reflection of my light, my truth, my power.
Many stories are told of me, but the one whispered most often is this:
Once, I hid myself away, retreating into the darkness of a cave, unwilling to shine. The world outside grew cold, lifeless, silent.
Without me, there was no day—only a heavy, endless night.
They say I left because I was wounded.
My own brother, wild and reckless, tore through my world with destruction, staining my light with his chaos. I could not bear to see my radiance cast upon ruin, so I withdrew.
I refused to shine for a world that did not honor it.
But the world needed me.
The gods, the spirits, and the people gathered outside my cave—calling, singing, pleading for my return.
When I peeked out, hesitant, uncertain, they held up a mirror, reflecting my own brilliance back at me.
And in that moment, I remembered—I was never meant to be hidden.
I stepped forward, and as I did, the world bloomed again.
The frost melted. The birds sang. The sky opened.
The light returned—because I had returned.

The birds sang.
The sky opened, and the light returned.
Because I had returned.
And now, I ask you, my love.
How long have you been hiding?
How long have you made yourself small, believing the world would be fine without your light?
Step forward.
Let them see you.
Let yourself see you.
Rise.

## THE MYSTERY OF AMATERASU- WHO IS SHE TODAY?

I walk this modern world today.
I am the golden glow that spills across your skin in the morning, the light that floods the streets after the storm, the warmth on your back when you turn your face toward the sun.
I see you, even when you cannot see yourself.
You will find me where the light touches the earth, where shadows retreat, where people are learning to embrace their own radiance once more.
In this time, I am an artist of light. A photographer. A storyteller. A woman who holds up the mirror and reminds others of what they have forgotten about themselves.
She stands before you now, lifting her camera with quiet precision, fingers adjusting the lens as the golden morning light filters through the leaves.
"There," she murmurs, tilting her head as she studies you. "That's the real you."
Her camera is not just a tool—it is an extension of her, a mirror held up to the world, revealing the beauty that has always been there.
She understands light better than anyone. She knows how to capture it, how to shape it, how to make it sing.
Because once, she lived in the dark.
She knows what it is to retreat, to believe that hiding is the only way to be safe.
She knows what it is to feel like the world will only take and take, until you have nothing left to give.
But she also knows what it means to step back into the light—to claim it, to let it illuminate everything she once thought she had to keep hidden.
"People don't always see their own light," she tells you, lowering her camera, her

gaze steady and sure. "But I see yours."

She lifts the camera one more time. The lens clicks.

And when she shows you the photo—when you see yourself bathed in golden light, glowing, powerful, whole—you finally understand.

You are Amaterasu.

And the world has been waiting for you to rise.

## AMATERASU'S RITUALS: RECLAIMING YOUR RADIANCE

To walk with Amaterasu is to step into your own light, to embrace visibility, and to own your space.

Her rituals are about self-worth, confidence, and radiance from the inside out.

Ritual #1: The Mirror of Light (For Confidence & Self-Recognition)

You will need:

A small hand mirror (symbol of Amaterasu's return to herself)

A gold or yellow candle (representing your inner light)

A quiet space with natural sunlight (to reflect your radiance back to you)

How to Use:

Light your candle and hold the mirror in front of you.

Look at yourself—not as you have been told to see yourself, but as you truly are.

Notice the details—the way the light touches your skin, the quiet strength in your eyes.

Whisper to your reflection:

"I am radiant. I am seen. I do not shrink—I shine."

Breathe deeply, feeling the warmth of the light on your skin, allowing it to sink into your bones.

Blow out the candle, carrying the light within you as you step back into the world.

# WHAT MESSAGE DOES AMATERASU WHISPER TO YOU?

Come, my love. Step into the light.
How long have you dimmed yourself for the comfort of others? How long have you made yourself small, believing that brightness is something to apologize for?
There is warmth within you that the world aches for.
There is brilliance within you that cannot be extinguished.
Do not mistake your power for arrogance.
Do not mistake your radiance for something that must be softened.
You are not too much. You are not too bright. You do not have to shrink to make others feel comfortable in your presence.
Shine, my love. Shine without hesitation.
Balance is not about making yourself less.
Balance is knowing when to rest and when to rise.
Balance is understanding that you do not have to be at full glow all the time—but you must never forget that you are the sun itself.
Even when I hide behind the clouds, I am still here.
Even when I set, I always return.

And so will you.
Rise, my love.

The world is waiting.

## The Sun & The Moon
## Embracing Both Sides

You have felt the sun on your skin.
You have seen yourself in the light.
But what of the shadows?
For too long, we have been told to choose:
To be strong or soft.
To be radiant or mysterious.
To be seen or felt.
But the goddesses teach us that we are both.
Amaterasu shows you the power of stepping forward, of reclaiming space, of illuminating the world around you.
But there is another power just as potent—the power of drawing inward, of surrendering to depth, of letting the world come to you.
Every goddess, every woman, carries both.
The Sun and The Moon.
Light and Shadow.
Radiance and Mystery.
One does not exist without the other.
You do not shine only in the daylight.
You do not draw others in only when you are golden and glowing.
There is beauty in the pause, in the moment before dawn, in the quiet magnetic pull of night.
Light draws people in.
Desire keeps them there.
Amaterasu stepped forward so the world could see her again.
Aphrodite does not step forward.
She waits.
She lets them come to her.
Now, it is time to enter the realm of desire.
Where in your life do you need to embrace your own glow?
And where do you need to surrender to your own depth?


Turn the page, my love. Aphrodite is waiting.

*I radiate love, beauty, and confidence.
My heart is open to abundance.*

**Aphrodite**
The Goddess of Love & Self-Care

## A WHISPER IN THE DARKNESS

Ah, my love… finally, you have come to me."
You stand before me, longing. Searching.
I see it in your eyes, in the way you hesitate, in the way you have been taught to ask permission before claiming what has always been yours.
But tell me—who told you that you must wait to be chosen?
Who told you that love is something to earn?
Who told you that beauty is something to prove?
You were not meant to shrink.
You were not meant to apologise for your softness, for your pleasure, for the way your body aches to be touched, worshipped, adored—first by yourself, and then by the world.
Look at yourself, my love. Truly look.
The curve of your lips. The line of your collarbone. The glow of your skin in the flickering candlelight.
You were sculpted by the gods, kissed by the sea, woven together with silk and stardust.
And yet, you have forgotten.
So let me remind you.

## I AM TOLD MY STORY GOES...

I am Aphrodite (Ἀφροδίτη)—the Goddess of Love, Beauty, and Desire.
They say I was born from the sea, from the foam where the heavens and the earth collided.
As I rose from the water, the world held its breath.
Flowers bloomed where my feet touched the shore.
The sky blushed with the first hues of dawn.
The gods themselves fell silent in my presence.
They worshipped me in Cyprus, Corinth, and Athens, offering roses, myrtle, and the sweet scent of incense.
They built temples and statues in my name, for they knew that beauty is not vanity—it is power.
But love is not always gentle.
My name has started wars.
My name has been whispered in jealousy, in longing, in devotion.
Men have fought for me.
Women have called upon me—desperate to be seen, to be wanted, to be enough.

And now, I see you.
You who have forgotten how to love yourself.
You who have been told your worth is only what others see in you.
"But do you not remember?
You are the sea.
You are the storm.
You are the rising tide, the hunger in your own bones."
"Let them look. Let them want.
But know this—you do not exist for their desire.
You exist for your own."
"Look at yourself.
See what I see."

# THE MYSTERY OF APHRODITE – WHO IS SHE TODAY?

I walk this modern world today.
You see me before you smell me.
And when you do, you ache.
Not for me. No—for yourself.
For the woman you have been too afraid to become.
The one who walks into a room and owns it.
The one who does not look away when she meets her own gaze in the mirror.
The one who whispers her name as if it is a spell, knowing that it is.
I am the woman in the perfume boutique, draped in pearls and velvet, a vision of silk and seduction.
The kind of woman who leaves a trail of roses and honeyed jasmine in her wake.
I lift a delicate crystal bottle, watching the golden liquid catch the light.
My fingers are slow, deliberate, teasing as I press the scent to your wrist.
"Close your eyes," I say, my voice like silk slipping off bare skin.
You do.
The scent curls around you, soft and sinful all at once.
Rose and vanilla, warm and decadent.
A whisper of amber, sultry and knowing.
The promise of lips grazing your collarbone, fingertips trailing down your spine.
"Breathe it in," I tell you.
"Let it sink into your skin, into your bones. Let it become a part of you."
You shudder.
"What do you want?" I ask.
You hesitate.

"No," I say gently, brushing a loose curl from your face.
"Say it. Say what you desire."
Your lips part.
And for the first time, you do.
Because this is what it means to be me.
To be wanted, adored, but never owned.
To be the one who chooses, not the one who waits to be chosen.
You are Aphrodite.
And the world is yours for the taking.

# APHRODITE'S RITUALS: SENSUALITY, SELF-WORSHIP & EMBODIED DESIRE

To walk with Aphrodite is to reclaim yourself—to see beauty not as something to be earned, but as something you already are.

### RITUAL 1: THE MIRROR SEDUCTION
(For Self-Love & Confidence)

A large mirror (a sacred reflection, a portal to self-reclamation)
A red or pink candle (symbol of passion and self-love)
A silk robe or something that makes you feel sensual

How to Use:

Light your candle and stand before your mirror. Let the glow illuminate your skin, your shape, your presence.
Run your hands over your body—not critically, not with judgment, but with gratitude.
Feel your curves, your edges, the warmth beneath your skin.
Whisper to your reflection:
"I am beauty. I am pleasure. I am enough."
Let the words settle in your bones. Breathe them in. Believe them.
Blow out the candle, leaving the warmth of Aphrodite's presence lingering on your skin.

### RITUAL #2: THE GODDESS PERFUME
(For Magnetism & Sensual Power)

3 drops rose essential oil (love, attraction, beauty)
2 drops vanilla extract (warmth, sweetness, indulgence)
1 drop jasmine oil (sensuality, confidence, feminine power)

A carrier oil (jojoba or almond oil)

How to Use:

Blend the oils together in a small vial.
Warm a drop between your fingers and press it to your pulse points—your wrists, your throat, your heart.
Close your eyes and inhale deeply.
Feel the energy shift—the way the air hums around you, the way your presence expands.
Whisper:
"I am magnetic. I am desire. I am irresistible."
Let the scent become a part of you—a signature, a statement, a promise to yourself.

## WHAT MESSAGE DOES APHRODITE WHISPER TO YOU?

"Stop waiting for love to find you."
"Be love. Become desire itself."
"You are not here to be modest. You are not here to be palatable. You are here to be radiant, magnetic, untamed."
"Look at yourself, my love. Touch your skin. Speak your name with reverence."
"You are Aphrodite."
"And the world is at your feet."

*I embrace my inner fire. My energy is fierce, bold, and unstoppable.*

Pele
The Goddess of Passion & Strength

# YOU WERE BORN TO BURN

You were not born to be tame. You were not meant to be quiet. You are fire—you burn, you create, you rise."
You are the heat beneath the surface.
You are the pulse in the earth, the hunger in your chest, the force that cannot be contained.
You are fire.
Not a flickering candle.
Not a controlled spark.
A roaring, untamed blaze.
And the world has tried to silence you.
They have called you too much.
Too loud.
Too intense.
Too wild.
They have poured water over your flame, expecting you to dim, to shrink, to disappear.
But fire does not disappear.
It waits.
It smolders beneath the surface, hungry, patient—until the moment it erupts.
"So tell me, my love—how long have you been waiting?"
"How long have you let others tell you to be small?"
"How long have you smothered your own flame for the comfort of others?"
"Enough."
"Burn. Burn until there is nothing left of what you were told to be, and only what you were meant to become."

# I AM TOLD MY STORY GOES...

In Hawaiian mythology, I am Pele, the Goddess of Fire, Volcanoes, and Passion.
They call me Pele-honua-mea—"Pele of the Sacred Land," for I shape the very bones of the earth itself.
I was born across the sea, but I could not stay still.
My spirit was restless.
My hunger—endless.
I traveled across the waters, carrying fire in my soul, searching for a land that could hold my power.
When I arrived in Hawai'i, I clashed with my sister, Namaka, the goddess of the ocean.
She tried to drown me, to smother my fire with her waves.

But I would not be silenced.
My flames raged against the sea, carving mountains from the deep, birthing islands from the void.
They say I am destruction—but they do not understand.
I do not burn for the sake of ruin. I burn for transformation.
My lava devours the old, but from the ashes, new land rises.
I am the protector of my sacred land, the guardian of those who honor it.
I do not tolerate disrespect.
I do not allow what is sacred to be taken without cost.
If you do not honor the fire, it will consume you.
"You do not smother fire, my love.
You learn to walk beside it, to wield it, to let it change you."

## THE MYSTERY OF PELE – WHO IS SHE TODAY?

I walk this modern world today.
The heat of the kitchen wraps around you like a second skin, the scent of spice curling in the air.
The woman before you moves with reckless grace, fire flashing in her dark eyes, her hands commanding the flames like they are an extension of her soul.
"You're holding back," she says, not looking up from the pan, where oil crackles and dances like embers in the wind.
You hesitate, the knife in your hand trembling slightly.
"Cut," she commands.
You obey, slicing through the ripe mango, its juices slick and golden beneath your fingertips. The blade moves with newfound confidence, the rhythm of the kitchen humming beneath your skin.
She grins, tossing a pinch of red chili into the fire.
You cannot create something unforgettable if you are afraid of the heat."
Her laughter is low, knowing—a sound that ignites something deep inside you.
She is more than a chef. She is a force of nature, a woman who builds, destroys, and builds again.
She does not apologize for the flames—she controls them.
She does not burn for destruction—she burns to protect, to cleanse, to make way for what must come next.
You meet her gaze, and suddenly, you understand.
You are not here to play small.
You are not here to simmer.

You are Pele.
And you were born to burn.

# PELE'S RITUALS: UNLEASHING PASSION, TRANSFORMATION & POWER

To walk with Pele is to step into the fire—to claim your desire, your anger, your hunger, and let it shape you into something unbreakable.

### RITUAL 1: THE FIRE OFFERING (For Letting Go & Rebirth)

**What You Need:**
A small fireproof bowl or dish (the container for your transformation)
Dried hibiscus or red chili flakes (symbols of Pele's passion and fire)
A slip of paper with something you need to release

**How to Use:**

Write down something you are ready to let go of—fear, doubt, hesitation.
Place the paper in the fireproof dish and sprinkle the dried hibiscus or chili over it.
Light a flame, watching as the fire consumes what no longer serves you.
Whisper:
"I burn away the old. I rise from my own ashes. I am fire."
Let the embers cool, then scatter the ashes outside, returning them to the earth.

### RITUAL 2: THE FIRE TONIC (For Energy, Passion & Strength)

**What You Need:**
1 cup hot water (activates the ingredients, awakens the senses)
½ tsp fresh ginger (grated) (fire, movement, circulation)
½ tsp cayenne pepper (heat, passion, boldness)
1 tbsp lemon juice (cleansing, transformation)
1 tsp raw honey (sweetness, balance)

**How to Use:**

Combine all ingredients in a mug.
Stir clockwise, calling in Pele's fire, her energy, her strength.
Hold the cup in your hands, feeling the warmth, the power, the promise of change.
Whisper:

"I drink fire. I become fire. I am unstoppable."
Sip slowly, letting the heat wake something inside you

## WHAT MESSAGE DOES PELE WHISPER TO YOU?

"You were not made to be still, to be silent, to be contained."

"You were made to erupt, to carve new paths, to set the world alight with your presence."

"Do not fear your own hunger. Do not fear your own power. Do not let them tell you that fire is dangerous when you were born to burn."

"You do not exist to be liked. You exist to be felt."

"I do not burn for destruction—I burn for creation. I burn for protection. I burn for the ones who have forgotten their own fire."

"So burn, my love. Burn until there is nothing left of what you were told to be, and only what you were meant to become.

## The Alchemy of Fire & Flow

You have burned. You have risen. Now, you create.
The fire has stripped you bare.
It has melted away the illusions, the limitations, the fear.
You have stood before the mirror and seen yourself in full—
You have stepped into the flames and emerged unbroken, unstoppable.
So, what comes next?
A goddess does not burn just to destroy.
She burns to make space.
To create.
To birth something new.
Close your eyes.
Breathe in the embers, the echoes of your own rising.
Feel it—the heat is still there, but now it moves differently.
It is no longer wild—it is purposeful.
It is no longer chaotic—it is focused.
It no longer rages—it flows.
This is where wisdom begins.
This is where you turn fire into art, into words, into expression.
This is where you step into flow.
The fire has opened the path—
Now, it is time to walk it.

Turn the page, and let Saraswati guide your hands, your voice, your art.

# THE CURRENT THAT CARRIES YOU FORWARD

They will tell you that wisdom comes from silence, that creativity is a gift you are given—
not a river you must follow."
They are wrong.
Wisdom is not something you wait for—it is something you chase, unravel, surrender to.
Creativity is not a luxury—it is the air you breathe, the water you drink, the current that pulls you toward your destiny.
And I am here to show you how to follow it.
Because the greatest mistake you have been taught is this:
That inspiration is something you must wait for.
That you must be still, passive, empty, until it decides to find you.
But tell me—
Does a river wait for permission to flow?
Does music wait to be heard?
Does the tide stop moving because the shore is not ready?
No.

"And neither should you."

I AM SARASWATI
I am the rhythm of words, the ink that spills onto paper,
the song that moves through your veins before you even know the melody.
I am the whisper of inspiration before the masterpiece,
the breath before the first stroke of paint,
the flood of clarity when the puzzle pieces finally fit.
I am wisdom, but I am not old.
I am knowledge, but I am not rigid.
I am flow—the endless, rushing, untamed river of knowing.
I do not stop moving.
I do not wait.
I do not hesitate.
I am the voice of creation itself.
And so are you.

# I AM TOLD MY STORY GOES...

In Hindu mythology, I am Saraswati (सरस्वती), the Goddess of Wisdom, Learning, Music, and the Arts.

My name means "the one who flows", for I am both knowledge and movement the sacred river of inspiration that never stops running.

They say I was born from Brahma's thoughts, pure and shining, wisdom in its most divine form.

I ride upon a swan, the bird that can separate truth from illusion, knowledge from ignorance.

My hands hold a veena, an instrument whose notes weave the fabric of existence itself.

I am the goddess of scholars, musicians, writers, poets, and seekers.

But my devotees do not kneel in temples.

They pick up their pens, lift their voices in song, and run their fingers over the keys of a typewriter,

a piano, a canvas waiting to be filled.

But make no mistake—

I do not sit still.

I do not wait for wisdom to be handed to me.

"I flow. I chase knowledge. I seek understanding.

I devour, I explore, I create."

"And so must you."

Because wisdom is not passive.

It is alive, moving, always reaching for the next great idea, the next masterpiece, the next discovery.

The only question is—

Will you let it carry you forward?

# THE MYSTERY OF SARASWATI – WHO IS SHE TODAY?

I walk this world of knowledge, creation, and limitless expression. The library hums with quiet energy, the scent of old books and fresh ink wrapping around you like a spell.

At the center of the room, a woman sits before an open book.

But she is not reading—she is writing.

The words spill from her pen in a rush, effortless, flowing like water.

She does not hesitate.
She does not question whether the words are right or wrong.
She simply trusts the movement.
You hesitate before speaking, but she looks up—already knowing.
"You are waiting for inspiration," she says, tapping the edge of her notebook.
You nod.
She smiles—kind, but sharp, like a blade hidden beneath silk.
"Then stop waiting."
She pushes the book toward you.
"Write the first word. Play the first note. Speak the first thought."
"Wisdom is not something you passively receive. It is something you must step into."
"So stop waiting, my love."
"Start creating."
You are Saraswati.
And you do not chase inspiration—you become it.

## SARASWATI'S RITUALS: CREATIVITY, LEARNING & UNLOCKING THE FLOW STATE

To walk with Saraswati is to step into your own creativity, to chase knowledge with hunger, to trust the current of inspiration when it calls.

RITUAL 1: THE FLOW STATE INVOCATION (For Writers, Artists & Thinkers)

You Will Need:
A blank page or canvas (the beginning of something brilliant)
A blue candle (Saraswati's color, the shade of wisdom and truth)
A mantra or phrase of intention (e.g., "I trust the process. I allow the flow. I am creativity itself.")

How to Use:

Light the blue candle, letting its glow remind you that all knowledge is already within you.
Place your hands over the blank page, whispering:
"Saraswati, guide my hands. Guide my voice. Let the ideas flow through me like a river."
Write, paint, or create—without stopping, without questioning. Let it pour from you.
When you are finished, whisper:

"I do not wait for inspiration. I create it."

RITUAL 2: THE MUSIC OF THE MIND (For Unlocking Intuition & Clarity)

You Will Need:
A quiet space with soft instrumental music playing (to mimic the flow of Saraswati's veena)
A cup of warm saffron or chamomile tea (soothing, stimulating the mind without overwhelming it)
A single question you need an answer to

How to Use:

Close your eyes, letting the music fill your mind, soften your thoughts, open the doors of knowing.
Hold your question in your mind—not forcing an answer, but allowing it to rise naturally, like a melody taking shape.
Sip the tea slowly, letting the warmth settle in your chest.
Whisper:
"I do not seek answers. I allow them to come to me."
Open your eyes and trust the first thought that enters your mind.

## WHAT MESSAGE DOES SARASWATI WHISPER TO YOU?

"You were not made to be still, to be silent, to be contained."
"You were made to erupt, to carve new paths, to set the world alight with your presence."
"Do not fear your own hunger. Do not fear your own power. Do not let them tell you that fire is dangerous when you were born to burn."
"You do not exist to be liked. You exist to be felt."
"I do not burn for destruction—I burn for creation. I burn for protection. I burn for the ones who have forgotten their own fire."
"So burn, my love. Burn until there is nothing left of what you were told to be, and only what you were meant to become.

## YOU STAND AT THE CROSSROADS

You stand at the threshold, trembling.
One path leads to the life you've always known—safe, familiar, but small. The other… the other is unknown, wild, terrifying.
But listen to me now—
You were not meant to stay where you are.
I Am Hecate
I am the shadow at the edge of your vision, the whisper in the wind when you cannot decide.
I am the torch that lights your way, the key that unlocks the door, the silent presence beside you when you stand at the crossroads of your life.
I am the beginning.
I am the end.
I am the space between.

## I AM TOLD MY STORY GOES…

In ancient Greek mythology, I am Hecate (Ἑκάτη), the Goddess of Magic, Witchcraft, the Moon, and the Crossroads.
They say I walk the boundaries between worlds—the living and the dead, the known and the unknown, the past and the future.
I was honored in Thrace and Anatolia long before the Greeks wove me into their myths. They called me the Keeper of the Keys, the Goddess of the Three Paths, the one who stands at the threshold between choices.
I was not like the Olympians. I did not demand temples or grand tributes. Instead, my offerings were left at the crossroads—garlic, honey, eggs, and black dogs, gifts to appease the restless spirits that wandered the in-between places, the ones I guided and protected.
But my most famous myth is whispered in the darkness—the story of Persephone.
When she was stolen into the underworld, it was I who heard her cries. It was I who carried my torches into the abyss, guiding Demeter through the black void in search of her daughter. I did not hesitate. I did not fear the dark. I walked between the worlds with my head held high.
And when the deal was struck—when Persephone was bound to both the sunlit world above and the shadowed realm below—it was I who stood by her side, teaching her how to rule the night as well as the day.
I am Hecate.
I do not fear the darkness.
I own it.

And now, I ask you—
Where are you afraid to go?
What path calls to you, but terrifies you all the same?
You are standing at the crossroads now.
I am here to tell you—choose.
It is time.

# The Mystery of Hecate: Who Is She Today?

I walk this modern world of liminality, moving between the seen and the unseen.
I am the one who knows before you speak, who sees before you decide.
The alleyway is dimly lit, the scent of night jasmine thick in the air. You hesitate outside the door, your pulse thrumming.
You have heard of her.
The fortune-teller, the tarot reader, the woman who never gives easy answers.
You exhale, pressing your palm against the cool metal of the door, and push it open.
Inside, a single candle flickers on a table draped in deep indigo. Smoke curls from a brass censer, the scent of myrrh and clove wrapping around you like unseen fingers.
And then—you see her.
A woman sits behind the table, dark eyes steady, the flickering light catching on the silver ring around her finger, the key dangling from her throat.
She does not smile.
"You have come with a question."
Her voice is low, rich with something ancient, something that knows.
She reaches for the deck of cards beside her and spreads them out, the edges worn, the images dark with promise.
"But you already know the answer."
She turns the first card.
The Crossroads.
She lifts her gaze to yours, and in that moment, you understand.
This was never about fate.
This was never about the universe deciding for you.
This was always about choice.
You are Hecate.
You are the one who decides.
And the world is waiting for you to step forward.

She does not hesitate.
She does not question whether the words are right or wrong.
She simply trusts the movement.
You hesitate before speaking, but she looks up—already knowing.
"You are waiting for inspiration," she says, tapping the edge of her notebook.
You nod.
She smiles—kind, but sharp, like a blade hidden beneath silk.
"Then stop waiting."
She pushes the book toward you.
"Write the first word. Play the first note. Speak the first thought."
"Wisdom is not something you passively receive. It is something you must step into."
"So stop waiting, my love."
"Start creating."
You are Saraswati.
And you do not chase inspiration—you become it.

# Hecate's Rituals: Walking the Crossroads of Change & Power

To walk with Hecate is to step into your own knowing—to claim your power, your path, your transformation.

Ritual 1: The Crossroads Spell (For Decision & Clarity)
A black candle (Hecate's guiding light at the crossroads)
A silver key (the key to unlocking your path)
Three slips of paper (each one representing a choice or fear)

How to Use:

Light the black candle and place the key beside it. This is your moment of decision.
Write down three things:
A path you are afraid to take.
A fear that keeps you frozen.
A version of yourself you wish to become.
Fold the slips of paper and hold them over the flame, feeling the heat, the power of choice.
Whisper:
"Hecate, Keeper of the Crossroads, light my path. I step forward with

clarity, with courage, with power."
Burn the papers in a fireproof dish, releasing your hesitation into the flames.
5. Carry the silver key with you as a talisman, a reminder that the power was always yours.

Ritual 2: The Moonlit Bath (For Transformation & Letting Go)

A bowl of warm water (the in-between, the space of change)
3 drops of mugwort oil (vision, intuition, Hecate's herb of the night)
1 tsp sea salt (purification, clearing old energy)
A black stone (obsidian or onyx) (absorbs fear, strengthens resolve)

How to Use:
Under the new moon or at midnight, prepare your bath or a small bowl of water.
Stir in the mugwort and salt, feeling the shift in energy as the water transforms.
Hold the black stone in your palm, whispering:
"I release what no longer serves me. I step into what I am meant to become."
Dip your hands into the water, pressing them to your chest.
When you are ready, pour the water onto the earth, returning the old to the night.

# What Message Does Hecate Whisper to You?

You are standing at the edge, hesitating.
You are waiting for a sign, for something to tell you which way to go.
But I am not here to tell you what to do.
I am here to tell you that you already know.
You can walk back to what is familiar, to what is safe.
Or you can step into the unknown, into your own power, into the life that has been calling you for longer than you realize.
I will not push you.
I will not decide for you.
I will only ask—

Are you ready?

*I honor my body's wisdom and embrace the power of natural healing*

Ixchel
The Mayan Goddess of Healing

# I AM THE WEAVING OF STORIES, THE HANDS THAT HEAL

I am the curve of the waning moon, the pull of the tides, the ebb and flow of all things.
I am the healer's touch, the whisper in the night, the hands that cradle both life and loss.
I am the sacred weaver, threading together the stories of women—their joy, their sorrow, their hopes, their heartbreak.
I have seen them kneel beneath the stars, praying for what may never come.
I have stood beside them in the quiet moments—
In the rooms where their dreams took their first breath,
And in the rooms where they did not.
I am the storm before the calm, the flood that cleanses, the soft hands that bandage wounds both seen and unseen.
I am the goddess who teaches that grief must be felt before healing can begin.
I am Ixchel.
And I am here for you.

# I AM TOLD MY STORY GOES...

In Mayan mythology, I am Ixchel, the Goddess of the Moon, Water, Healing, Fertility, and Rebirth.
I am the one women have turned to for centuries—those who long for life in their womb, those who have birthed and lost, those who seek the kind of healing that cannot be seen.
They say I was once a radiant maiden, my beauty so luminous that even Kinich Ahau, the Sun God, was captivated by me.
He pursued me, burned for me, loved me—but the sun's love is not always gentle.
His jealous rage struck me down, his lightning carving its mark into my very being.
I lay lifeless for days, the world holding its breath.
But the creatures of the earth gathered around me—the serpents, the jaguars, the hummingbirds—whispering their magic, their wisdom, their knowing.
And so, I rose again.
I was no longer the same.
I left the sun behind.
I took my place beside the moon, choosing the path of cycles, of transitions, of endings and beginnings.
From the heavens, I watched over the women, the healers, the mothers, and the

ones who could never be.

They came to me in temples on Cozumel and Isla Mujeres, leaving offerings of jade and water, whispering their hopes into the night.

But not all prayers are answered.

Not all wombs swell.

Not all love stories end with lullabies and laughter.

I have seen women clutch their empty hands, kneel beneath the moon, and wonder if they are broken.

And I have whispered back—

"No, my love. You are not broken at all."

## The Mystery of Ixchel: Who Is She Today?

In this world today, I am the one who pours your drink.

The café hums softly, the scent of cinnamon and rain curling through the air.

You sit alone, fingers tracing the rim of your cup, staring at the tea leaves swirling in the bottom—searching for answers, for something, for anything.

You did not come here for the drink.

You came here for the silence.

And then—I am here.

I do not announce myself.

I do not press you for conversation.

I simply set your cup down and say, "Are you okay?"

You look up, startled.

And something inside you cracks.

Not because of the words, but because no one has asked you that in a long time.

Because you have spent so much time holding it together, carrying the weight of what was never spoken.

I see it in your eyes.

The grief. The unspoken pain. The longing for something that feels just out of reach.

I know.

Because I have carried it too.

I do not tell you everything happens for a reason.

I do not offer meaningless reassurances.

Instead, I sit beside you.

I let the moment stretch between us—soft, fragile, unspoken.

"Drink," I say.

And so you do.

And in that quiet space, as the warmth fills you, as your breath slows, as the

storm inside you settles just a little—
You realize: you are not alone.
You are Ixchel.
And you are still whole.

## Ixchel's Rituals: Healing, Rebirth & Honoring What Was Lost

To walk with Ixchel is to honor your pain without letting it consume you.
To acknowledge what is missing while remembering what is still here.

Ritual 1: The Moonlit Offering (For Closure & Peace)

A bowl of water (Ixchel's sacred rivers, the flow of emotions)
White flowers (jasmine, chamomile, or lily—symbols of grief, purity, release)
A small silver object (ring, coin, charm—symbol of the moon, of things unseen but still felt)

How to Use:

Place the bowl of water in the moonlight, letting it reflect the silver glow.
Whisper into the water the name of what you are releasing—a dream, a person, a part of yourself.
Drop the silver charm into the bowl, watching as the ripples carry your sorrow away.
Lay the flowers on the water's surface and whisper:
"I honor what was. I embrace what is. I open my heart to what will be."
In the morning, return the water and flowers to the earth, releasing the past with it.

Ritual 2: Ixchel's Healing Tonic (For Emotional & Physical Restoration)

1 cup warm almond milk or herbal tea (nourishing, calming)
1 tsp honey (sweetness, comfort, restoration)
½ tsp chamomile flowers (or tea bag) (soothing, healing, release of tension)
A pinch of cinnamon (warmth, protection, energy to move forward)

How to Use:

Warm the almond milk or herbal tea, stirring in the honey, chamomile, and

cinnamon.
Hold the cup in your hands, letting the warmth sink into your bones, your breath slowing.
Whisper:
"I do not rush my healing. I do not force my journey. I allow myself to grieve, to rest, to rise."
Sip slowly, knowing that healing is not about forgetting—it is about finding strength in what remains.

# A Message from Ixchel: To Every Woman Who Has Ever Felt Not Enough

"I have heard your prayers. The whispered ones. The desperate ones. The ones you never dared to speak aloud."
"I have seen the way you watch other women, the way your heart clenches even when you do not want it to. I know the sting of smiling while someone else cradles what you have longed for."

"I know the way you carry grief, folded neatly inside you, tucked away where no one else can see it. The way you pretend you are fine. The way you tell yourself you should not feel this way, because others have it worse, because you should be stronger, because you should not let it hurt so much."
"But, my love—"
"You are allowed to grieve."
"You are allowed to feel the ache of something you cannot have."
"You are allowed to wonder what might have been."
"But do not let it make you feel less than whole."
"You are not incomplete."
"You are not unworthy."

"You are not less of a woman because your path has taken a different turn."
"Motherhood is not the only way to create. You have brought love into this world in a thousand ways."
"You are doing enough."
"You are enough."

"And if you are the woman who has chosen not to bear children, do not let the world tell you that you are missing something. You are sovereign in your own body, your own choices, your own path. You do not owe the world an explanation for the way you choose to exist."

"I am Ixchel."
"I have granted life, but I have also held loss."
"And still—I rise. Still, I heal. Still, I carry on."
"And so will you, my love."
"You are not broken."
"You are still whole."

# THE ICE QUEEN OF STRENGTH & INDEPENDENCE

You were not made for softness alone. You were not made to be kept warm in another's shadow. You were made for the wild, for the frost-kissed winds, for the sharp bite of independence that sings in your veins."
I Am Skadi
I am the crisp bite of winter air, the whisper of snow beneath your feet, the stillness of a world frozen in time.
I am the huntress who moves through the storm without hesitation, the force that does not beg to be understood.
I am the one who stands alone—and is not afraid.
You will not find me in warm halls, nor waiting at the hearthside for another to call me home.
My home is the mountain, the ice, the sky stretched wide and endless above me.
I am the cold that does not kill, but sharpens.
I am the solitude that does not isolate, but empowers.
I do not ask permission.
I do not seek approval.
I take what is mine.
I am Skadi.
And I am waiting for you to stand beside me.


# I AM TOLD MY STORY GOES...

In Norse mythology, I am Skadi, the Giantess of Winter, the Huntress of the Mountains, the Goddess of Independence and Vengeance.
They call me the one who walks alone, the one who chooses her own fate.
They say I was born among the Jotun—the frost giants, the ancient beings of ice and stone.
I was not made for softness, nor for the gilded halls of gods who feared the wild.
But when the Aesir killed my father, I did not weep.
I did not plead.
I took up my bow.
I marched to Asgard—not as a beggar, but as a warrior demanding retribution.
The gods, taken aback by my rage, tried to pacify me.
They offered me gold, jewels, riches beyond measure.
But I did not want wealth—I wanted justice.

So I made my demand.
I would choose a husband from among the gods.
But not by face.
No—by their feet.
They laughed, but they agreed, believing I would be satisfied.
I gazed at the line of gods before me, their faces hidden, and selected the most beautiful feet among them.
I believed them to belong to Balder, the radiant god of light.
But when the veil was lifted, I saw I had chosen Njord, the god of the sea.
A man of salt and waves, a god of warmth and water, utterly unlike me.
And so, I tried.
I tried to live by the shore, where the sun melted my beloved ice.
I tried to love the waves as much as I loved the mountains.
I tried to be what he wanted.
But love cannot be forced.
So I did what few women have ever done.
I walked away.
I left my husband, left the halls of gods, and returned to the mountains where I belonged.
I chose myself.
And I did not regret it.
"Do you hear me, my love?"
"You do not have to stay where you do not belong."
"You do not have to shrink yourself to fit into another's world."
"You do not have to settle for anything less than your own wild, beautiful life."
"Come with me."
"There is freedom waiting for you in the snow."

## The Mystery of Skadi: Who Is She Today?

I walk this modern world today.
The cold air stings your face as you step onto the trail, your breath rising in clouds before you.
Your boots crunch against the snow, the quiet hum of the wilderness wrapping around you like a cloak.
She is waiting.
The woman beside you moves with confidence, a bow slung across her back, a wolfish grin curving her lips.
She is your guide, but she does not lead—she walks beside you, a silent challenge in the sharpness of her gaze.

You don't need permission to be strong," she says, adjusting the strap of her pack.
"Strength is already in you. You just have to stop apologizing for it."
You hesitate.
"You're afraid of standing alone?" she asks.
"Why?"
The question catches in your throat.
She laughs, but it is not unkind.
"You are already alone, my love. You've just been pretending you aren't."
You look up, watching as the wind moves through the trees, as the snow glows beneath the pale light of the moon.
And suddenly, you understand.
There is no shame in solitude.
No fear in strength.
No guilt in wanting more.
She lifts her bow, aims, and looses an arrow.
It soars through the air, sharp, precise, unflinching.
"You are Skadi," she whispers.
"And you were born to walk your own path."

## Skadi's Rituals: Strength, Solitude & Choosing Yourself

To walk with Skadi is to choose yourself unapologetically.
It is to know your worth without seeking validation.
It is to claim your freedom, your independence, and your right to walk away.

Ritual 1: The Solitude Walk (For Strength & Clarity)

A pair of boots or shoes that make you feel powerful (grounding, independence)
A cold morning or evening air (sharpens the mind, awakens the senses)
A single question to reflect on (What am I holding onto that is keeping me small?)

How to Use:

Step outside alone. Walk with purpose. Let the cold bite your skin, let the wind whip through your hair.
Breathe deep—feel the clarity that comes with solitude.
Whisper:
"I am strong. I do not need permission to exist as I am."

5, Keep walking, keep breathing, keep choosing yourself
.

Ritual 2: The Cold Water Strength Test (For Resilience & Power)
A bowl of ice water or a cold shower (shock, awakening, resilience)

A deep inhale, a slow exhale (control, power, discipline)
A single word—your strength word (Freedom? Power? Fearless?)

How to Use:

Submerge your hands in the ice water. Let the cold seep into your skin, testing your resolve.
Focus. Do not flinch. Do not pull away.
Whisper:
"I do not run from discomfort. I do not fear change. I am Skadi."
Remove your hands. Dry them. Stand tall.
The world does not break you.
The world sharpens you.

# What Message Does Skadi Whisper to You?

You are afraid to be alone.
"But you have always been alone. You just did not want to see it."
"Now, see it. Own it. Do not shrink yourself for comfort. Do not stay where you do not belong. Do not let the fear of solitude keep you from your own power."
"Strength is not found in the arms of another. It is found in the way you stand when there is no one beside you."
"I do not tell you to walk alone forever."
"I tell you to walk alone until you know, truly, that you are not afraid to."
"Then, my love, you will never settle again."
"You are Skadi."
"And the mountains are calling."

# Honoring the Tears
# Before the Transformation

Before fire. Before ice. Before rebirth—there are tears.
We do not always talk about this part.
The part where grief holds us in its quiet hands.
The part where dreams are mourned before they are replaced.
The part where the weight of what we have lost is too heavy to carry alone.
And yet, we must feel it before we can move forward.
Ixchel knew this.
She was the goddess of healing, but healing is not a quick remedy.
It is not a soft hand that makes the pain disappear.
It is a storm.
It is rain that drowns the earth before it nourishes it.
It is allowing the grief, the ache, the longing to exist—without shame.
For every woman who has lost.
For every woman who has held emptiness where life was meant to be.
For every woman who has mothered in ways the world does not recognize.
For every woman who has felt like she was never enough—
Ixchel is with you.

You do not have to rush this.
You do not have to "get over it" before you are ready.
You are allowed to sit with your sorrow before you stand again.

So before we move forward, before we step into transformation—breathe.
If you have cried, know that you are not alone.
If you have wept, know that your tears are seen.
There is power in grief.
There is power in honoring what was lost.
And when you are ready—when you are truly ready—
We will step forward.
Together.

The next goddess awaits.

# THE GODDESS OF STORMS & THE DEATH OF THE OLD SELF

The storm is not your enemy. The ending is not your downfall. The cold is not your punishment. It is your rebirth."
I Am Cailleach.
I am the last breath of winter, the wind that strips the trees bare.
I am the death of what no longer serves you, the storm that washes away what you are too afraid to release.
I am the Old Woman of the Winds, the Veiled One, the Winter Queen.
I am the end.
And because of me—you begin again.

# I AM TOLD MY STORY GOES...

In Celtic mythology, I am Cailleach, the Crone Goddess of Winter, Storms, and Transformation.
My name means Veiled One, for I am the keeper of secrets, the force that moves unseen, the power that arrives in the dark of the year when all things must sleep.
I was here before the gods, before the druids, before the first fire was ever lit in the hearth.
I have walked these lands for a thousand winters, shaping the mountains with my staff, calling the snow with a whisper, forging rivers from ice and stone.
They say I rule from Samhain to Beltane, from the first chill of autumn to the first bloom of spring.
I am the darkness before the dawn.
And yet—I am not cruel.
For without death, there is no rebirth.
Without loss, there is no space for something greater.
Without the storm, there is no clear sky.
"And now, I ask you—what are you clinging to?"
"What part of yourself is withered, broken, dead—but you are too afraid to let it go?"
"Winter is coming, my love. And it is time."

## The Mystery of Cailleach: Who Is She Today?

I walk this modern world not to take, but to clear the way.
I walk where others fear to tread.
I am the force that strips away the old, the unnecessary, the illusions you have clung to for too long.

I do not bring death—I bring truth.

The storm rages outside, wind howling against the windows, rain hammering against the roof.

Inside, the woman before you moves with unshaken ease, the glow of the fire casting shadows across the lines of her face.

Her hands are weathered—hands that have built, hands that have buried, hands that have let go.

She stirs the cauldron before her, the scent of mugwort and rosemary thick in the air.

"You're afraid of endings," she says, not looking up.

The words settle in your chest, an unspoken truth you have been running from.

She ladles a steaming cup into your hands, the liquid dark as the storm outside.

"Drink."

You hesitate.

"If you wish to stay where you are, set the cup down. Walk away. Keep holding on to what no longer fits you."

She finally looks up, her eyes gleaming like iron in the firelight.

"But if you are ready to let the old self die—then drink, and step into the storm."

Your fingers tighten around the cup.

And you lift it to your lips.

You are Cailleach.

And the past no longer owns you.

## Cailleach's Rituals: Releasing, Rebuilding & Becoming Something New

To walk with Cailleach is to accept the storm—to let the winds strip you bare, to allow the old to fall away, to step into what you were always meant to be.

Ritual 1: The Burning of the Old Self (For Release & Transformation)

You Will Need:
A piece of paper (a written farewell to the self you are leaving behind)
A fire-safe bowl or cauldron (Cailleach's forge of endings and new beginnings)
Dried rosemary or pine needles (cleansing, purification, cutting ties to the past)

How to Use:

Write down who you are releasing—an old version of yourself, a fear, a belief

that no longer serves you.
Sprinkle the dried rosemary or pine over the paper, whispering:
"I honor what was. I release what is no longer mine. I step into what is waiting for me."
Burn the paper, watching the smoke rise, carrying the past away with it.
Scatter the ashes in the wind, returning them to the storm.

Ritual 2: The Ice Bath of Rebirth (For Strength & Renewal)

You Will Need:
A bowl of ice water (the frozen waters of transformation, the last breath of winter)
A black stone (obsidian, onyx, or tourmaline—grounding, facing the unknown)
A deep, silent place (preferably outside in the cold air)

How to Use:

Place your hands in the ice water, feeling the shock of cold, the sensation of release.
Hold the black stone, whispering:
"I do not fear the storm. I do not fear what I must leave behind. I rise from this winter anew."
Remove your hands, feeling the warmth return—a reminder that you always survive.
Keep the stone as a talisman—a promise that endings are not to be feared, but rather, the first breath of something greater.

# What Message Does Cailleach Whisper to You?

"You cling to the old self, though it no longer fits you."
"You resist the storm, though it is the only thing that will clear your path."
"Let go."
"Let it break."
"Let the wind tear it away, let the frost take what no longer belongs to you."
"And when the storm has passed—"
"You will stand, unshaken, untouched, reborn in the silence that follows."
"Do not fear the winter, my love."
"For you were always meant to rise from it."

## The Throne You Stand Upon

Power is not something given—it is something taken.
It is built, fought for, risen into.
Some will tell you that you must earn your place, that power is a reward for obedience, for playing the game by their rules.
But tell me—who designed those rules?
Cleopatra did not wait to be handed a kingdom—she claimed it.
Cailleach did not beg for change—she brought the storm.
And now, my love—it is your turn.
They will tell you to be softer, quieter, more likable.
They will tell you that power is dangerous in the hands of a woman.
Let them talk.

# THE QUEEN WHO NEVER DIES

"They have written a thousand stories about me."
"Some call me a seductress, a temptress, a woman who wielded power through beauty alone. But tell me—"
"If beauty was all I had, why do they still fear my name?"
I Am Cleopatra.
I am the pulse beneath a nation's skin, the steel wrapped in silk, the whisper of a woman who has never once bowed.
I am the gold that glints in the sun, the scent of myrrh thick in the air, the strategy sharper than any blade.
I am power that does not ask permission.
I am the empire they could not erase.
I am the ruler who did not wait to be chosen—because I chose myself.
I was the last pharaoh of Egypt.
And yet—I never truly left.

# I AM TOLD MY STORY GOES...

In Egyptian history and mythology, I am Cleopatra VII Philopator—the last ruler of the Ptolemaic Kingdom, the living embodiment of Isis, the queen who stood against an empire.
I was not just a ruler.
I was Egypt itself.
They have tried to shrink me into a legend of men and desire, as if my name was merely an echo in the halls of conquest.
They call me a seductress because they could not admit that a woman could hold power without a man's permission.
They call me a lover of great men because they refuse to acknowledge that I was the greatest of them all.
But my story did not begin with Rome.
It began with the gods.
My people called me the Daughter of Ra, the New Isis, a queen whose reign was blessed by the divine.
I was not just a woman—I was a force, a sovereign ruler who understood that power is not inherited—it is taken, wielded, and shaped by those who dare to claim it.
They say I spoke a dozen languages, that I did not need interpreters to rule my land.
I negotiated treaties, restructured Egypt's economy, commanded armies, and

rebuilt a crumbling empire when the world expected me to fall.
They tell you about the men who stood beside me, but they do not tell you that I was the one who made the world kneel.
They do not tell you about the woman who fought for her throne—not once, but three times.
They do not tell you about the queen who turned the wealth of a dying kingdom into a legacy that would outlast her conquerors.
They do not tell you about the ruler who refused to bow.
And when my kingdom fell, when the Romans claimed my land as their own, they believed they had erased me.
They believed my story ended with an asp's bite.
They believed history would remember me only as a woman who loved too deeply.
But I ask you now—
Does that sound like the end of my story?
Or does it sound like the beginning of something else?
"What if the snake was never meant to kill me? What if it was simply the symbol of my transformation?"
"What if I never truly died at all?"
"What if I am still here—rising, adapting, whispering my name into the bones of history, reminding the world that I was never theirs to bury?"
"Look at yourself, my love. You think your power is gone, but you are only in your cocoon."
"Shed the skin that no longer fits you."
"Rise again."

## The Mystery of Skadi: Who Is She Today?

I walk this world today, not as a relic, not as a memory—but as a force.
My power does not fade.
My legacy does not belong to the past.
I am written in the bones of every woman who refuses to be forgotten."
The skyline of Cairo stretches before you, golden light spilling over rooftops.
You step onto the balcony, the silk of your robe cool against your skin, the weight of gold at your throat—a talisman, a reminder.
The woman beside you moves with effortless grace, adjusting the gold-rimmed glasses perched on her nose.
She is power incarnate, a CEO, an empire builder, a woman who does not ask for permission to take up space.
"Do you know why they still speak of me?" she asks, swirling dark coffee in her

cup, her voice rich, edged with something timeless, undeniable.

You shake your head.

She smiles—slow, knowing.

"Because I never left."

She leans forward, studying you, her gaze like the Nile—ancient, unmoving, powerful.

"You think you are small. You think you are fragile. But I see the way you move. I see the way they watch you when you enter a room."

She lifts a single brow.

"You remind me of someone."

You swallow, heart pounding, unsure if you should feel flattered or afraid.

"You think you were born to live quietly, to let others decide your fate?" she asks, tilting her head.

"My love, you were born to rule."

The weight of the gold around your neck feels heavier now.

You meet her gaze.

And suddenly, you understand.

You are Cleopatra.

And you never die.

## Cleopatra's Rituals: Power, Influence & Unapologetic Rebirth

To walk with Cleopatra is to step into your power, to command your own empire, to never be reduced to what others say you are.

Ritual 1: The Golden Bath (For Self-Worth & Magnetism)

You will need:
A bath infused with milk & honey (the legendary beauty secret of queens)
Rose petals (love, seduction, sovereignty over one's own desires)
Gold flakes or shimmer oil (luxury, opulence, the embodiment of power)

How to Perform the Ritual:
Prepare your bath, infusing the water with milk, honey, and rose petals.
Add gold flakes or shimmer oil, watching as the water glows around you.
As you sink into the bath, whisper:
"I am wealth. I am wisdom. I am unforgettable."
Let the warmth soak into your skin, absorbing Cleopatra's legacy.
Step out of the bath and anoint yourself with perfume, marking yourself as

royalty in your own right.

Ritual 2: The Power Sigil (For Influence & Strategy)

You will need:
A blank page & pen (to write your own legacy, not let others write it for you)
A gold candle (the fire of strategy, power, and presence)
A piece of jewelry (ring, necklace, or bracelet—a talisman of confidence and influence)

How to Perform the Ritual:
Write down the three qualities you want to be remembered for.
Light the gold candle, tracing your initials into the wax.
Whisper:
"I am remembered. I am a force. I do not fade—I rise."
Fold the paper and place it beneath your chosen piece of jewelry.
Wear this talisman whenever you need to channel Cleopatra's energy.

# What Message Does Cleopatra Whisper to You?

"They will try to erase you."
"They will rewrite your story."
"They will reduce your name to whispers and rumors."
"Let them."
"For you are still here."
"You are not simply history—you are legend."
"And legend never dies."

## The Empress Walks Forward

Some say power is about legacy—about being remembered.
But Cleopatra does not ask if history remembers her.
She knows it does.
Because power is not about how the world sees you—it is about how you see yourself.
It is not about being feared.
It is about never fearing yourself.
It is not about being given a crown.
It is about wearing one—without needing permission.
So before you turn this page, ask yourself

What throne do I hesitate to claim?
What empire am I afraid to build?
What story am I allowing others to write for me?

Stop waiting.
Stop shrinking.
The world is already yours.
Now—walk like you remember that.

## I TAKE. I COMMAND. I OWN EVERY INCH OF MY POWER

They say love makes you weak. They say beauty is a weapon—but only when wielded against you. They say a woman who desires is a woman who can be controlled."

"Let them say it."

"Then watch as I ride into battle with roses in my hair and blood on my hands."

I Am Freyja.

I am the golden glow of desire, the warmth of hands pressing against silk, the hunger that drives kings mad.

I am the war cry that splits the sky, the blade hidden beneath a lover's whisper, the predator's patience before the kill.

I am beauty and death, hunger and restraint—the hand that caresses your cheek just before I take what is mine.

And I have never asked for permission.

## I AM TOLD MY STORY GOES...

In Norse mythology, I am Freyja ("Lady"), the Goddess of Love, War, Wealth, and Magic. A daughter of the Vanir, wilder than the Aesir, older than Odin's rule.

They say my tears turn to gold when they fall. That I ride a chariot pulled by great cats, my cloak woven from falcon feathers. That when warriors die, half of them come to me before Odin takes his share for Valhalla.

They whisper of my Brísingamen—the necklace so powerful I traded my nights to obtain it.

But do they tell you that it was not submission, but a bargain?

That I never surrendered—I simply knew my own worth.

They call me a lover, a wife, a mother.

But they forget I am also a commander, a sorceress, a queen in my own right.

"They have tried to separate the parts of me that make them uncomfortable—"

"But I am all of it. And I refuse to be made small."

"They say you must choose—fierce or feminine, warrior or lover, bold or beautiful. But I say—why not both?"

"You do not have to shrink to fit their idea of who you should be. You do not have to apologize for being too much."

"You are Freyja. And too much was never enough for you."

## The Mystery of Freyja: Who Is She Today?

I walk this world today, and I own every step I take.

My heels click against polished marble floors, the weight of the room shifting the moment I enter.

Heads turn—not just because of my beauty, but because of something else, something undeniable.

I am the woman who sells you the dream before you even realize you want it.

A penthouse suite with a skyline view? You will swear you can already hear the champagne cork pop.

A mansion by the sea? The scent of salt and luxury is already in your lungs.

The house you thought you'd never have? I hand you the keys, and suddenly, it was always meant to be yours.

I do not convince you.

I do not persuade you.

I command the space until you are ready to follow.

And when the deal is signed—when you have spent more than you planned, and you do not regret a single cent—I leave you in the doorway, still spellbound by the vision I placed in your mind.

And then?

You'll find me in the VIP lounge of a high-rise bar, a crystal glass in my hand, the city skyline glinting in my golden earrings.

Across the room, I see you hesitating. Watching. Wanting.

I smirk and tip my glass.

An invitation? A challenge? A dare?

You hesitate for only a moment—then you cross the room, drawn in before you even realize you've moved.

I don't look up immediately. I let the tension linger. Let the space between us hum with possibility.

Then, I speak.

"They say women like us are dangerous."

I swirl the drink in my hand, slow, deliberate. The ice clinks against the glass—a heartbeat, steady, controlled.

"They say we are too much—too bold, too confident, too ambitious."

I lean in, voice low, dripping with knowing.

"Tell me, my love—have you ever been tempted to apologize for the way you take up space?"

You swallow, unsure.

I smirk.

"Don't."

From my purse, I draw something—a delicate golden necklace, the weight of history and power embedded in its shine.

I hold it between two fingers, watching it catch the light, before sliding it across the marble table to you.

They will tell you that you must choose—be desirable, or be powerful. Be soft, or be strong. Be adored, or be respected."
I tilt my head.
"I did not choose."
"I took it all."
Your fingers tighten around the necklace, the cool metal burning against your palm.
I watch you, waiting. Will you wear it?
Because if you do—you will never be the same again.
I smirk once more, lifting my glass.
"Wear it when you're ready to remind them who you are."
You are Freyja.
And you were never meant to ask for power.
You were meant to own it.

# Freyja's Rituals: Power, Magnetism & The Art of Taking What You Deserve

To walk with Freyja is to embrace your full self—unapologetically, sensually, without hesitation.

Ritual 1: The Red Lipstick Spell (For Confidence & Commanding Presence)
A bold red lipstick (the war paint of queens, the symbol of unshaken confidence)
A gold mirror (for reflection, power, and self-admiration)
A single phrase of intention: "I do not ask. I take."

How to Use:

Stand before the mirror, holding the lipstick in your palm.
Whisper:
"I am magnetic. I am irresistible. I am Freyja."
Apply the lipstick, watching as your reflection transforms into something bold, undeniable, unforgettable.
Step into the world, knowing that you do not beg, do not chase—you simply are.

Ritual 2: The Battle Perfume (For Unstoppable Charisma & Attraction)
3 drops of rose oil (love, seduction, self-admiration)

2 drops of cinnamon oil (passion, fire, confidence)
1 drop of black pepper oil (fearlessness, power, taking what is yours)
A base of jojoba or almond oil (smooth, grounding, long-lasting presence)

How to Use:

Blend the oils in a small vial.
Warm a drop between your fingers and press it to your pulse points—your wrists, your throat, your heart.
Whisper:
"I am desired. I am adored. I am unstoppable."
Walk into the world knowing that the air itself hums with your presence.

## What Message Does Freyja Whisper to You?

"You think you must choose—be strong, or be soft. Be loved, or be feared. Be admired, or be respected."
"But tell me—why do you limit yourself?"
"The world is already yours. The only question is, will you reach out and take it?"
"You are not too much. You are exactly as you were meant to be."
"You are Freyja."
"And you have always known your worth."

# THE ICE QUEEN OF STRENGTH & INDEPENDENCE

"They tell my story in whispers, in myths softened by time. They say I was selfish. That I reached too high. That I took what was not meant for me."
"But tell me, my love—when has the world ever allowed a woman to choose her own fate without consequence?"
I Am Chang'e.
I am the silver glow of the autumn moon, the light that lingers just beyond your reach.
I am the longing in your chest, the dream that slips through your fingers the moment you wake.
I am the price of desire, the hunger for more, the reckless beauty of a wish made too soon.
I am the woman who loved, who lost, who rose beyond the limits of this world.
And now, I watch from above.

# I AM TOLD MY STORY GOES...

In Chinese mythology, I am Chang'e (嫦娥)—the Goddess of the Moon, the one who flew too high and never came back down.
They say I was once mortal, a woman who lived in the world of men. My husband, Hou Yi, was a great archer, the hero who saved the world by shooting down the ten suns that burned the earth. As a reward, he was gifted the Elixir of Immortality—a single draught that could lift one person to the heavens.
But the gods are cruel.
They do not grant gifts without burden.
And so, the elixir was not meant for two.
Some say I stole it. That my hands trembled as I drank, my heartbeat frantic with guilt.
Some say I was forced, that I had no choice but to take it before it fell into the wrong hands.
Some say I was selfish.
But what they never say—
Is that I was a woman with a dream. A woman who knew there was more. A woman who wanted more.
And so, the moment the elixir touched my lips, my body became weightless. The earth fell away beneath me, and I rose, my heart breaking as I drifted beyond the reach of the only love I had ever known.
They say I landed on the moon, where I now reside in a palace of cold jade and silver light.
They say I am alone, with only the Jade Rabbit, my eternal companion, to keep

me company.

They say I spend my nights looking down upon the world I left behind, longing for what I can never touch again.

But tell me—if I had stayed, if I had chosen the life laid out for me, would they have sung my name for centuries?

"They call me tragic. They call me foolish. But I ask you now—"

"What dream have you abandoned out of fear?"

"What part of you is still waiting to take flight?"

"What if you were never meant to stay small?"

"Look at the moon, my love."

"Do you think she regrets rising?"

## The Mystery of Chang'e: Who Is She Today?

In this world today, I am a High-Fashion Model and Designer—a woman draped in silk, walking as if gravity does not apply to me. My presence is effortless, ethereal, yet undeniable.

You see me before you understand me.

The glow of moonlight reflected in iridescent fabric, the whisper of silk trailing behind me like mist. I do not follow trends; I set them. I do not chase the spotlight; it turns to find me.

At the grandest fashion house, behind the heavy velvet curtain, I stand before the mirror. A gown of silver and pearl clings to my form, delicate as moonlight, untouchable as the sky.

A designer—one of the world's most revered—hovers nearby, adjusting the fabric with reverence. He does not speak. He knows better than to disrupt the silence that belongs to me.

"You always seem like you're somewhere else," he murmurs, not expecting an answer.

I meet his gaze through the mirror. A slow, knowing smile curves my lips.

"That's because I am."

I have walked among the stars. I have tasted eternity. I have known a love so great it became legend.

But I do not grieve.

I embody longing, not because I am incomplete, but because I understand that beauty is found in what cannot be touched.

At the gala, they whisper when I pass.

"She is untouchable."

"She moves like she is made of light."

"Who is she?"

I do not stop to answer.
They call me a muse, an enigma, a vision woven from silver thread. But the truth is simpler than that.
I am Chang'e.
I am the one who left everything behind and still became something divine.
I do not chase—I am the thing they seek.
And so are you.

## Chang'e's Rituals: Reaching Higher, Embracing Change & Owning Your Desires

To walk with Chang'e is to honor your ambitions, to accept that growth comes with sacrifice, and to never apologize for wanting more.

Ritual 1: The Flight of the Phoenix (For Courage & Bold Choices)

A piece of jade or a silver pendant (a talisman of transformation & protection)
A candle (white or silver) (symbolizing clarity & direction)
A written dream or goal you have been too afraid to chase

How to Use:

Light the candle, letting the soft glow remind you of the moon's quiet strength.
Hold the jade or silver pendant in your palm, feeling its cool, grounding presence.
Whisper:
"I do not fear my own potential. I do not shrink for the comfort of others. I rise, as I was always meant to."
Write down the dream or desire that has been waiting inside you.
Fold the paper and tuck it beneath the pendant, keeping it close to your heart.
Let this be your reminder: You are allowed to want more. You are allowed to take flight.

Ritual 2: The Moonlit Tea Ceremony (For Reflection & Letting Go of Regret)

1 cup jasmine tea or white tea (delicate, floral, linked to clarity & intuition)
1 tsp honey (gentle sweetness, acceptance of change)
A quiet space with a view of the moon

How to Use:

Brew the tea, letting the fragrance fill the air.
Sit beneath the moon or by a window where its light touches your skin.
Hold the warm cup, breathing in the steam, feeling the weight of the past melt away.
Whisper:
"I release what no longer serves me. I embrace the path that calls me forward. I trust the journey ahead."
Drink slowly, allowing each sip to ground you in the present, in your own power, in the beauty of what's to come.

## What Message Does Chang'e Whisper to You?

"They have told you that wanting more makes you selfish."
"That rising higher makes you greedy."
"That stepping beyond what is expected of you will leave you alone."
"But tell me—"
"Do you think the moon cares when they call her distant?"
"Do you think she hesitates before rising?"
"No, my love."
"She simply ascends."
"And so will you."

# SHE DOES NOT CHASE, YET SHE IS ALWAYS FOLLOWED

The world tells you that you must shine like the sun—bright, loud, undeniable. But tell me, my love, have you ever noticed the way people whisper their secrets to the moon?"
"There is power in quiet. There is magic in mystery. And there is beauty in the glow of those who do not need to be seen to be felt."
I Am Selene.
I am the silver glow upon your skin in the dead of night.
I am the tide that pulls at your heart, the breath of wind that shifts the world in silence.
I am the dreamer's guide, the poet's muse, the lover's confidante.
I am the secret you keep even from yourself.
I am the Moon.
And I have always been watching.

# I AM TOLD MY STORY GOES...

In ancient Greek mythology, I am Selene (Σελήνη)—the Goddess of the Moon, the One Who Watches from the Heavens. My name means "light", but not the kind that burns—it is the kind that soothes, that reveals, that illuminates what is hidden.
They say I drive a chariot of silver and pearl across the night sky, pulled by shining white horses, casting my glow over the sleeping world.
They say my touch makes the tides rise, my presence stirs the dreamer's mind, my whispers bring visions in the night.
But the story they love most? Endymion.
A shepherd so beautiful, so untouched by time, that I fell in love with him. They say I begged Zeus to grant him eternal sleep so I could watch over him forever.
They say I loved him too much, that I could not bear to let him age, to let him slip from my grasp.
So I watched over him as he slept, his face forever bathed in my light.
But what they do not tell you—is that I have never feared solitude.
"I have always been alone, but I have never been lonely."
"They say I am quiet, that I am gentle, that I am soft. They forget that even in my stillness, I pull the tides. That I shift the earth beneath them without a single sound."
"I do not demand to be seen. But I am always felt."
"And so are you."

# The Mystery of Selene: Who Is She Today?

The city hums beneath you, the neon glow of streetlights reflecting off rain-slicked pavement. The world is awake, alive, but you are not part of its rush.
You sip your Earl Grey tea, infused with lavender and honey, letting the warmth settle in your bones. The café is quiet, the chatter around you distant, a murmur beneath the weight of your own thoughts.
Across from you, she watches.
She does not push for conversation. She does not interrupt the stillness.
She is a writer, a dreamer, a woman who moves through the world without needing to announce herself.
"People tell you that you should be louder," she says, stirring her tea with slow precision.
"That you should push, fight, burn."
She shakes her head, a slow, knowing smile curving her lips.
"But the moon does not shout. And yet, every night, the world turns its face toward her."
You say nothing, but she sees the shift in your eyes.
"You think your quiet makes you small. It does not."
"It makes you powerful."
She tilts her cup toward you, a silent toast to your knowing.
"There is magic in the things we do not say."
"And there is power in being the one who listens."
You are Selene.
And you do not need to be loud to be unforgettable.

# Selene's Rituals: Intuition, Beauty & the Power of Stillness

> To walk with Selene is to embrace your quiet strength, your soft magic, your deep knowing.

Ritual 1: The Moonlit Mirror (For Intuition & Self-Discovery)

A small mirror or reflective surface (a portal to the self, a channel for lunar wisdom)
A white candle (Selene's soft glow, a guiding light in the dark)
A silver ring or piece of jewelry (a talisman for intuition and dreams)

How to Use:
Light the white candle and hold the mirror in the moonlight.

Look into your own reflection—not with judgment, but with curiosity.
What do you see? What have you been avoiding?
Whisper:
"I see myself as I am. I trust the wisdom within me. I am the moon."
Wear the silver ring as a reminder that you do not need to be loud to be powerful.

Ritual 2: The Lunar Elixir (For Dreaming & Deep Rest)

1 cup warm milk (or herbal tea of choice) (soothing, calming, a drink of the night)
1 tsp honey (soft sweetness, lunar energy, comfort)
½ tsp lavender or chamomile (gentle dreams, connection to the subconscious)

How to Use:

Warm the milk or brew the herbal tea, stirring in honey and lavender.
Hold the cup in both hands, breathing in the steam.
Whisper:
"I trust the path that unfolds in the dark. I listen. I understand. I dream."
Sip slowly, allowing your mind to soften, your body to rest, your intuition to awaken.

# What Message Does Selene Whisper to You?

"They have told you that power is loud. That you must shout to be heard, that you must fight to be seen."
"But tell me—who do the lost call for in the dark?"
"They do not cry out for the sun."
"They turn their faces toward the moon."
"You are not forgotten. You are not unseen. You are the whisper that lingers, the light that softens the night, the tide that pulls the ocean without a single word."
"You do not need to demand their attention."
"They will look for you anyway."
"Because you are Selene."
"And the world always turns toward you in the end."

# The Final Whisper – The Goddess Within You

The stories have been told. The torches have been lit.
Now, the path is yours to walk.
You have stood in the fire with Pele, burning away what no longer serves you.
You have claimed your beauty and power with Aphrodite, daring to love yourself first.
You have embraced wisdom with Saraswati, allowing inspiration to flow through you.
You have chosen your fate with Hecate, stepping bravely into the unknown.
You have risen like the sun with Amaterasu, refusing to stay hidden in the dark.
You have wept with Ixchel, honoring the grief that shaped you.
You have ruled with Cleopatra, unshaken in your worth.
You have let go with Cailleach, trusting the storm to clear your path.
You have walked between love and war with Freyja, knowing you do not have to choose.
You have surrendered to Selene, embracing the quiet, the mystery, the knowing.
You have allowed Yhi to wake you, reminding you that you were always meant to rise.
Each goddess has left her mark upon you—not as something separate, something distant, but as a reminder.

You have never been just one thing.
You are not a single story.
You are the embodiment of all of them.

Because these goddesses were never just myths.
They were never just names in old stories, whispers in forgotten temples.
They were women who refused to be erased.
They were forces that could not be ignored.
They were power, rebirth, love, rage, creation, destruction, and everything in between.
And so are you.
Because these stories are not just theirs.
They are yours.

You are the fire that will not be tamed.
You are the tide that reshapes the shore.
You are the moon that commands the night.
You are the queen who will never be erased.

And when the world tries to make you small, when doubt creeps into your bones, turn back to these pages.
Let the goddesses remind you.
Let them stand beside you as they always have.

Let them whisper their power into your ear.
And then—go and live it.
This is not the end.

This is where you rise.
This is where you begin.

## The Goddess Cycle – Returning to the Thirteen

This book was never meant to be read once and set aside.
The goddesses do not call to you only once.
They whisper to you again and again—in different ways, at different times, through different seasons of your life.
Each time you return, you will find something new.
A lesson you were not ready for before.
A truth you had to grow into.
A message you could not hear until now.
Because you are always becoming.
And they are always waiting for you to return.

When You Need to Stand in Your Power...
Cleopatra – To command respect, refuse to be erased, and take up space without apology.
Freyja – To own your desirability and your ferocity—to be soft and sharp, lover and warrior.
Amaterasu – To step into the light, reclaim your radiance, and stop hiding.

When You Need to Let Go & Transform...
Cailleach – To strip away what no longer serves you, to embrace endings as the beginning of something greater.
Hecate – To stand at the crossroads and trust yourself to choose the right path.
Pele – To burn away the old and step fully into the new, unafraid.

When You Need Healing & Self-Love...

Ixchel – To grieve, to release, to find peace in the things that could not be.
Aphrodite – To love yourself first, to see your own beauty, to stop seeking permission to be adored.
Selene – To honor your quiet strength, trust your intuition, and embrace the stillness.

### When You Need Creativity, Wisdom & Flow…
Saraswati – To awaken inspiration, trust your ideas, and stop waiting—start creating.
Yhi – To break free from stagnation, wake up, and breathe new life into yourself.
Ixchel – To find beauty in what was lost and weave something new from the threads of your past.

### When You Feel Lost & Need Guidance…
Hecate – To see in the dark, walk into the unknown, and trust the whispers inside you.
Selene – To move in your own rhythm, be patient, and allow life to unfold in its own time.
Amaterasu – To remember that after every darkness, there is always a rising sun.

### The Goddess is a Cycle, Not a Destination
You are never just one of these goddesses forever.
You move through them, shifting between their lessons, their strengths, their wisdom.
Some days, you will be Aphrodite, radiant and irresistible.
Other days, you will be Cailleach, clearing the old and making way for what is next.
Sometimes, you will feel lost like Hecate, uncertain of which way to turn.
And in those moments, Selene will remind you to trust the mystery, to let the answers reveal themselves in time.
Because you are not meant to stay the same.
You are meant to evolve, transform, expand—again and again

# The Ache Before Healing
# The Pain Before Power

There is a kind of pain that no language can name.
The ache of emptiness, of longing, of love that had nowhere to go.
The grief of a dream that never came to life, of a door that never opened.
The silent sorrow of watching others hold what you have prayed for—and smiling through it.
There is a pain that lives in the spaces between words, in the rooms that were never filled, in the names that were never spoken.
And yet—the world does not make space for this grief.
They will tell you:
"You will move on."
"Everything happens for a reason."
"You were never meant for that path anyway."
But Ixchel knows better.
She knows the weight of love that could not take form.
She knows the silent cries spoken only to the moon, the prayers whispered into the dark.
She knows the agony of being the healer who cannot heal herself.
She is the goddess of birth—but she is also the goddess of what is never born.
She is the bringer of life—but she also holds the hands of those who mourn the lives that never came.
And so, she does not tell you to move on.
She does not tell you to be grateful for what you do have.
She does not tell you that time will erase the ache.
She only tells you this:
Your pain is real.
Your grief is valid.
You are not broken.
And you do not have to carry this alone.
She sits beside you in the quiet.
She holds space for the tears, the rage, the exhaustion of pretending to be okay.

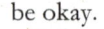

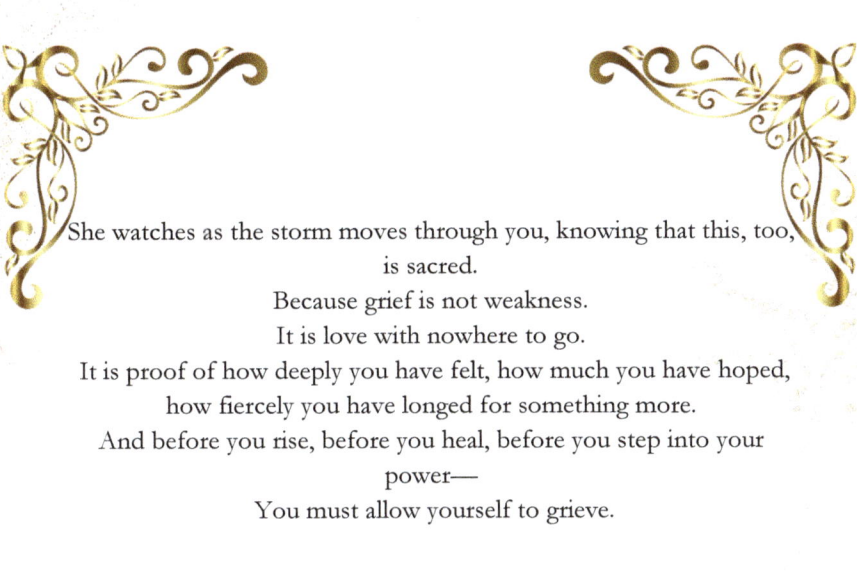

She watches as the storm moves through you, knowing that this, too, is sacred.
Because grief is not weakness.
It is love with nowhere to go.
It is proof of how deeply you have felt, how much you have hoped, how fiercely you have longed for something more.
And before you rise, before you heal, before you step into your power—
You must allow yourself to grieve.

## The Ritual of Release – Letting the Ache Speak

To walk with Ixchel is to honor your grief without letting it consume you.
It is to say, "I see you. I feel you. And I release you—bit by bit, in my own time."

A bowl of water (symbol of Ixchel's sacred rivers, the flow of emotions)
A white flower (for the loss, for the love, for the unspoken goodbyes)
A candle (to hold space for what could have been)

How to Use:

Sit in a quiet place. Place the bowl of water before you.
Hold the white flower in your hands, pressing it to your heart.
Whisper the words you have never said aloud—the ones that ache in your bones.
"I loved you before you ever arrived. I dreamed of you before I even knew your name.
And though you are not here, you are still real.
You mattered. You mattered to me."
Drop the flower into the water. Let the ripples carry your pain.
Watch as the petals float, as they drift—not gone, but changed.
When you are ready, pour the water onto the earth.
Let the ache return to where all things are transformed.
You do not have to let go all at once.
You do not have to forget.
You only have to breathe.
And when you are ready—you will rise.

# The Goddess Rebirth Ritual – Claiming Your Power

this is your moment.
You have walked through fire with Pele.
You have stood at the crossroads with Hecate.
You have embraced your beauty with Aphrodite.
You have risen with Amaterasu, and you have surrendered to the quiet glow of Selene.
You have seen yourself in these goddesses. Not as something separate—but as something you have always been.
Now, it is time.
To step fully into your own power.
To claim the name that has always been yours.
To stop waiting to become—and simply be.

Step One: Name Yourself
If you were a goddess, what would you be called?
Write it down. Whisper it. Own it.
Would you be The Goddess of Fierce Love?
Would you be The Goddess of Boundless Power?
Would you be The Goddess of Soft Strength, of Shadows, of the Wild?
You do not have to fit into a name you were given. You get to choose.

Step Two: Define Your Power
The world has tried to tell you who you are.
It has tried to shape you into something small, something quiet, something easy to understand.
But you are not here to be understood. You are here to be felt.
So write it down: What is your power?
Not what the world says.
Not what you have been told to be.
But what you know in your bones.
Are you the fire that refuses to be tamed?
Are you the stillness that cannot be shaken?
Are you the storm that clears the path, the hands that heal, the voice that commands?
You already know the answer.
Now, write it. Speak it. Believe it.

Step Three: Burn the Name the World Gave You
Take a piece of paper.
Write down the version of yourself that you are leaving behind.
The doubts. The hesitations. The fear that you are not enough.
The words that have been used to shrink you, to tame you, to keep you small.
And then—light the flame.
Watch the fire consume it. Watch the smoke rise. Watch it disappear.
Because you are no longer waiting to become.
You are already here.

Step Four: Step Into Your Goddess Power
Morning – Wake with Yhi. Take a deep breath. Feel the first light on your skin.
Midday – Walk with Cleopatra. Hold your head high. Speak like a queen.
Evening – Sink into Selene's glow. Light a candle. Journal. Whisper your dreams.
Live your power every single day. Not just in ritual. Not just in moments of confidence.
Every breath. Every step. Every choice.
You do not need permission.
You do not need to wait.
You are.

The Final Whisper
"They will try to tell you who you are. But you already know."
"They will try to define your power. But you have already claimed it."
"They will try to bury your voice. But you have already begun to rise."
"Now go."
"Walk like the goddess you were always meant to be."

# The Power Map – How to Live Goddess Energy Every Day

You do not need to wait for a moment of transformation. You are already becoming.

Power is not a thing that happens to you. It is a thing you choose. Every day.

Each goddess you have met lives within you. Some will call to you in moments of strength. Others will rise when you need to remember who you are.

This is how you weave their energy into your daily life.

MORNING: Wake with Yhi
The Goddess of Awakening & Light
Open your eyes with intention.
Take one deep breath. Feel the air fill your lungs like the first inhale of a new day.
Stand in the sunlight, even for a moment, and whisper:
"I rise. I am ready."
Drink water first thing—honoring Yhi's gift of vitality and life.
For when you need renewal. For when you feel stuck. For when you must begin again.

MIDDAY: Walk with Cleopatra
The Goddess of Power & Influence
Hold your head high. Command every space you enter.
Speak clearly, with certainty—your voice is not a question, it is a statement.
Make one bold decision today—whether in business, in boundaries, in how you carry yourself.
Adorn yourself in a way that makes you feel like royalty. Perfume, jewelry, a tailored jacket—something that makes you feel like a ruler.
Before stepping into a meeting, a room, or even just facing yourself in the mirror, whisper:
"I do not ask. I take."
For when you need confidence. For when you feel unseen. For when you must remind the world who you are.

EVENING: Sink into Selene's Glow
The Goddess of Lunar Beauty & Deep Knowing
Light a candle or let the moonlight touch your skin.
Journal—let your thoughts flow, free and unfiltered. The moon does not judge, and neither should you.

Take a warm drink before bed, something soft—chamomile, warm milk, honey-infused tea.

Reflect on your day: What did you learn? What did you feel? What secrets did the quiet moments reveal?

Close your eyes and whisper:

"I trust the path that unfolds in the dark."

For when you need peace. For when your mind is loud. For when you must remember that wisdom comes in whispers.

## CYCLE THROUGH THE GODDESSES AS YOU NEED THEM

Need to reclaim your sensuality? Walk with Aphrodite. Let yourself be desired—by yourself, first.

Need to burn away the past? Stand with Pele. Do not fear the fire—you are the fire.

Need to trust the unknown? Call on Hecate. The path does not need to be clear for you to step forward.

Need to let go? Sit with Cailleach. Winter does not kill—it clears the way for spring.

Need inspiration? Sing with Saraswati. Creativity is not a luxury—it is your nature.

## THE GODDESS ENERGY REMINDER

Place a symbol of your chosen goddess where you will see it. A ring, a stone, a phrase on your mirror.

Let it remind you:

You are not waiting to step into your power. You are already there.

# The Goddess Quiz – Which Goddess Are You Today?

The Goddess Quiz – Which Goddess Are You Today?
This book is a living, breathing guide.
You are never just one thing.
Some days, you need fire. Other days, you need softness.
Sometimes, you need to destroy and rebuild, and other times, you need to trust the flow of life.
The goddess you are drawn to today is the one whose power you need most.
Take the quiz. Let her guide you.

Which statement resonates with you the most right now?
A: I want to feel beautiful in my own skin. I want to embrace pleasure, love, and desire without apology.
B: I want to break free. I am tired of waiting, of hesitating. I need fire. I need movement.
C: I am done making myself small. I want to be powerful, to take up space, to stand in my own strength.
D: I do not need to be loud to be strong. I want to trust the quiet power within me, to follow my own wisdom.

Which of these emotions is strongest in you today?
A: Desire, longing, sensuality
B: Restlessness, hunger for transformation
C: Strength, independence, setting boundaries
D: Mystery, intuition, the need for stillness

When you look in the mirror, what do you need to see in yourself today?
A: A radiant, confident beauty who owns her own worth
B: A wildfire—unafraid to burn away the past and create something new
C: A warrior queen who bows to no one
D: A quiet force of nature who moves with patience and power

What is blocking you right now?
A: Doubt in your own attractiveness, charm, or ability to be desired
B: Fear of letting go, of change, of stepping into the unknown
C: Worry that if you don't hold everything together, it will all fall apart
D: Feeling disconnected, unseen, unsure of your next step

How do you want to feel?
A: Magnetic, irresistible, adored
B: Free, burning, unshaken
C: Strong, untouchable, completely in control
D: At peace, connected to something deeper

# Your Goddess Revealed

Your Goddess Revealed
Mostly A's – You are Aphrodite.
The Goddess of Love, Sensuality & Self-Worth
You are craving confidence, pleasure, and unapologetic self-love.
You need to see yourself through the eyes of desire—your own first.
What to do next: Adorn yourself. Take a mirror ritual. Whisper:
"I am magnetic. I am irresistible. I am enough."

Mostly B's – You are Pele.
The Goddess of Fire, Passion & Transformation
You are ready to burn away the past and rise anew.
You need courage, raw energy, and the ability to step fully into change.
What to do next: Write down what you are letting go of. Burn it. Whisper:
"I do not fear the fire. I am the fire."

Mostly C's – You are Cleopatra.
The Goddess of Power, Influence & Strategy
You are stepping into unshakable confidence and unstoppable success.
You need to own your presence, command respect, and take what is yours.
What to do next: Stand tall. Speak clearly. Take one bold action. Whisper:
"I do not ask. I take."

Mostly D's – You are Selene.
The Goddess of Intuition, Mystery & the Quiet Power of the Moon
You do not need to be loud to be powerful. You are meant to move in silence, to trust your own deep knowing.
You need stillness, wisdom, and connection to your own intuition.
What to do next: Sit in the moonlight. Hold water in your hands. Whisper:
"I trust the path that unfolds in the dark."

*Return to the Goddess You Need Most*
*If your results change tomorrow, let them. The goddess you need will always shift.*
*If two answers felt right, read both. You are more than one thing.*
*If no answer fits, flip to a random goddess chapter. The one who appears is the one calling you.*
*You are never just one goddess. You are all of them.*

My love,
I know why you are here.
I know what it feels like to be lost, to wonder if you will ever feel whole again.
To question whether you are enough—whether you have ever been enough.
I know what it feels like to stand at the crossroads, aching for a sign, a whisper, a torch to light the way.
To carry wounds that the world does not see.
To smile when your heart is breaking.
To dream of something more but feel trapped in a life that no longer fits you.
I know because I have been there too.
If you cried while reading this book, know that I cried while writing it.
Because we have all been there.
We have all needed to be reminded of who we are.
So let me remind you now:
You are not broken. You were never broken.
The world has tried to quiet you.
It has tried to shrink you.
It has tried to make you doubt your own magic.
But, my love, you do not belong in the shadows.
You were always meant to shine.
The goddesses you met in these pages? They are not distant myths.
They are not whispers of the past.
They are here.
They are you.
You are the fire of Pele.
You are the power of Cleopatra.
You are the beauty of Aphrodite.
You are the wisdom of Saraswati.
You are the resilience of Ixchel.

You are the moonlit strength of Selene.
You are the storm and the silence.
The beginning and the end.
The lover and the warrior.
The creator and the destroyer.
The one who chooses.
The one who rises.
The one who remembers.
And when you forget?
Turn back to these pages.
Let the goddesses remind you.
Let them whisper their truth into your bones.
And if the world ever makes you doubt your own power, if you ever feel lost again, come back to these words:
I am powerful. I am radiant. I am divine.
And most of all—I am never alone.
With love,
Yourself.